THE CLIMATE AND STATISTICS OF CONSUMPTION.

A PAPER READ BEFORE THE
AMERICAN GEOGRAPHICAL AND STATISTICAL SOCIETY

BY HENRY B. MILLARD, M.D.

MEMBER OF THE SOCIETY.

WITH EXTENSIVE ADDITIONS BY THE AUTHOR.

NEW-YORK:
WILLIAM RADDE, 300 BROADWAY.

WM. RADDE, 635 Arch Street, Philadelphia.—OTIS CLAPP, Boston.—R. & H. LUYTIES, St. Louis.—
HALSEY & KING, Chicago.—J. M. PARKS, Cincinnati.—JOHN B. HALL, Cleveland.
BALLIERE, 219 Regent-st., London.—TURNER, 97 Picadilly, Manchester.

1861.

Henry Ludwig, Printer and Stereotyper, 39 and 41 Centre Street.

TO

JOHN F. GRAY, M.D.,

THIS LITTLE VOLUME

IS

RESPECTFULLY AND GRATEFULLY

Dedicated.

PREFACE.

In the preparation of the following pages, the author has endeavored to present in a concise form, the results of the most valuable investigations in regard to the existence of consumption under the various and numerous circumstances in which it occurs, and, in connection with them, such comments and explanations as he thought might be useful and interesting.

As the disease in question is one which seems immutable in its character, he has made use of whatever information and statistics he has regarded as reliable, without reference to their newness; though, at the same time, he has spared no exertions to obtain the most recent facts and reports in reference to it, and has constructed as many new and original tables as the material within his reach would permit.

In two or three instances, paragraphs, particularly in reference to climate, have been taken almost literally from medical reviews, without reference being made to the source whence they were derived.

In conclusion, among many who have extended facilities to him towards the completion of his work, the author begs to return his grateful acknowledgments to W. WHELAN, M. D., Chief of the Bureau of Medicine and Surgery, U. S. Navy, Washington, D. C., HENRY I. BOWDITCH, M. D., Boston, Mass., and JAMES R. WYNNE, M. D., of New-York.

HENRY B. MILLARD.

28 EAST TWENTY-EIGHTH STREET,
New-York, December 1, 1860.

Contents.

THE CLIMATE

AND

STATISTICS OF CONSUMPTION.

Of the various departments of statistics none is of greater importance than that which relates to the records of mortality. Prosperity is checked, for the time, in its advancing march when men fall victims by thousands to epidemics; and familiar diseases, desolating households in their insidious progress, often palsy individual effort. Upon physical well-being is dependent prosperity, and through communities and individuals the ruddy tide of health must flow, for the intellect and energies to accomplish their best achievements.

There are certain facts pertaining to the nature, causes, and treatment of diseases, in regard to which the limited experience of a single individual, no matter how varied his opportunities, nor how correct his judgment, can have but little weight; but which can be determined only by statistics drawn from large masses of cases, embracing extended periods of time, and derived from various localities. Thus accumulated, medical statistics constitute one of the strongest safeguards of public health. Presenting, with terrible distinctness, to our eyes, the ravages of death, otherwise half unnoticed and unsuspected in their extent, which are ceaselessly going on in our midst, they render us more solicitous and more on the alert for our safety; and demonstrating the influence of climate, of age, of atmospherical conditions, and employments in the production of disease, aid us in understanding its causes and nature, and thus furnish us, to a certain extent, with weapons for protection. Mr. J. C. Kennedy, in his interesting paper on statistics, read before this society, remarks: "Were the preventable deaths which annually occur in this city of New-York to take place in any one week, they would throw a pall over every street and lane, and strike such a terror into the minds of the people as to paralyze industry and stagnate trade." This, too, "Apart from the consideration involved in the great amount of preventable sickness (not unto death) whereby such a vast amount of labor and earnings are lost and misery inflicted."

Besides, these stern battalions of facts do no little service in destroying theories relative to the nature and treatment of disease, often worse than harmless, and more the offspring of fancy than the fruit of reason, into which the practitioners of a somewhat uncertain art are often tempted and led astray, while venerated theories of centuries' growth have received their death-blow from an array of a few simple figures.

No disease has given rise to so many and such varied theories concerning its character and treatment as consumption, and in none other, from its nature and importance, can statistics be expected to be of greater use. In regard, first, to—

I.—The General Prevalence of Consumption.

It has been estimated that about one-sixth of all the deaths among the human race occur from this disease. This estimate, large as it may appear, seems still larger when we consider that it refers, not simply to the deaths among adults, but includes, also, those occurring during infancy—a period by far the most fatal of our existence. In New-York city it destroys about one-third more lives than all the other diseases of the respiratory organs together—as bronchitis, congestion and inflammation of the lungs, catarrh and influenza, whooping cough, croup, and asthma. Compared with the mortality it occasions, the ravages of war and famine, the devastations of the plague, cholera, and yellow fever, seem insignificant. No climate exempt from its sway, no age from its grasp—exercising its relentless rule in the frosty climes of the North, in the scorching heats of Africa, and in the more genial atmosphere of the Temperate Zones—it plants its fatal seeds alike in the bosom of the unborn babe, of the tender infant, and in the frame of the man trembling on the extreme verge of old age.

These facts prompt us to inquire under what principal conditions the deaths from consumption occur: under what varieties of climate; whether it is most prevalent on sea or on land; at what seasons it is most fatal; its comparative prevalence in city and country; the influence of light and darkness upon its existence; its prevalence among the various races and among the various callings and conditions of mankind; among the two sexes, and at the various periods of life. And here I would state that, in using the word *consumption*, I refer to that variety of phthisis characterized by a deposition of tubercles in the respiratory organs—the ordinary phthisis pulmonalis of writers.

There have been various estimates of the mortality from this disease: one writer attributing to it a third part of all the deaths in the world; most staticians, however, placing it at a little less than one-sixth of the entire mortality.

Dr. Caspar, in 1847, from a table of 60,000 deaths, occurring from various diseases and within a period of 20 or 30 years, in Berlin, Paris, Stuttgart, Philadelphia, Hamburg, London, Boston, and Baltimore, found the ratio of deaths by consumption to the deaths by other diseases as 1 to 5.8.

In a table recently constructed by myself, of 2,771,728 deaths from all diseases, occurring at various times between the years 1804 and 1860, in England and Wales, Paris, St. Helena, Algiers, Boston during a period of 35 years, Portsmouth, Baltimore, in the United States Army for 13 years, Charleston for a period of 25 years, Brooklyn, Memphis, Chicago for 8 years, the Canton of Geneva, Berlin, Salem, New-Orleans, Russia, Italy, New-York city for 57 years, Limerick, Philadelphia for 10 years,—I find that 483,588 deaths, or 1 in 5.7, were caused by consumption—the ratio agreeing very nearly with that obtained by Dr. Caspar.

These estimates, formed as they are from deaths occurring in almost every variety of climate, and in almost every accessible latitude, and comprising every class of people, might be considered as giving the true proportion of deaths from this disease. Probably they are nearly accurate estimates of the mortality from consumption in civilized countries during the last 50 years; but they cannot be considered exact as regards the mortality from the disease throughout the whole world, since there are countries in which, as we shall see, consumption is quite unknown, and some cities in which it prevails even more extensively than in any of those from which we have derived our estimate, either of which, if included, might considerably modify it.

II.—Its Present, Compared with its Former Prevalence.

It would be interesting to compare the present mortality from consumption with that which existed in ancient times, and to trace its progress and watch the fluctuations in its increase and decrease down to the present day. Unfortunately, though the disease is fully treated of by the Latin and Greek medical writers, they give no exact accounts of the *extent* of its prevalence, and we are obliged to satisfy ourselves with the conclusion that it was then, as now, one of the most common and formidable of maladies.

The science of medical statistics is one of very recent origin, and, in judging of the comparative prevalence of consumption now and in early periods, we have, to assist us in forming conclusions, only isolated returns from large cities, few of them extending farther back than fifty years. There is, however, no reason for supposing, the world over, that there has been, unless within the last 10 or 15 years, any material increase or diminution of the disease for centuries. The returns of the city of London, which have been kept for 230 years, show that, from 1629 to 1740, it caused a 6.6 part of all the deaths; while from 1740 to 1830 it caused a 4.6 part, or nearly a third as many more. During the first period, the mortality amounted, in nine years, to no more than a ninth part, ranging from that to one-fourth; during the last, varying from one-sixth to one-third. It seems to have increased from 1700 to 1830, causing, at the beginning of this period, one twenty-second part, and at the close, one-third of the deaths. Since 1830 the deaths have seldom exceeded a sixth part of the whole. From the year 1847 to 1858, however, out of 607,676 deaths by consumption, 70,135 (11.5 per cent., or only 1 in 8.6) were from consumption: a ratio which might lead us to suppose that the disease was on the decline in that city, had there not been, as was stated above, at one time during the period between 1629 and 1740, a still smaller proportion—namely, 1 in 9.

A similar diminution in the amount of the disease seems to have existed throughout all England and Wales during the same period, the deaths from consumption being generally estimated at a little more than one in six; from 1838 to 1843 the proportion being 1 in 5.4. From 1847 to 1858, out of 4,526,747 deaths, it caused 559,974—12.3 per cent., or only 1 in 8. It is probable that this vast diminution in the amount of the disease during the last 10 years is not entirely of a transitory character, but that, as is certainly very much to be hoped, it has its basis, in part, at least, in improved sanitary measures, in a better understanding of the nature, and, consequently, a more intelligent treatment of the disease.

In New-York city, from 1804 to 1820, the deaths by consumption were 1 in 4.2; from 1820 to 1835, 1 in 5.4; from 1835 to 1850, 1 in 6.5; and from 1848 to 1859, 1 in 8.46. These figures, however, do not give the exact proportion of the increase and decrease of the disease in New-York and London, as the relative mortality undoubtedly depends very much on the diminished or increased mortality from other diseases. There is no doubt, however, that in New-York it has steadily declined since 1805. In Boston, from 1810 to 1818, the ratio of deaths by consumption was about 1 in 7; after that there was a gradual decrease of the disease till 1845, when it caused about 1 death in 6.5.

III.—Its Prevalence in the United States and England Compared.

Of the 2,777,728 deaths mentioned above, 716,819 occurred in the United States; of these 117,879 (16.4 per cent., or 1 in 6.08) were by consumption. As this table is, however, made up principally from returns from cities—unlike the English returns, into which enter the reports of all the rural districts—it cannot be regarded as furnishing the exact proportion of deaths by consumption in the United States. According to the mortality reports of the United States census for the year 1850, the deaths by consumption that year were 33,576, or 1 in 9.63. Owing, however, to the imperfect and faulty system of registration which exists in our country, these data furnished by the census probably cause as great a deviation from the exact proportion as existed in the first estimate. The vast majority of the deaths entering into the first estimate occurred before the year 1850. Perhaps a diminution in the amount of the disease throughout the country may account for something of the discrepancy.

In England and Wales, as has been mentioned, the total number of deaths from 1838 to 1843 was 1,634,435, of which 1 in 5.4 were by consumption; from 1847 to 1858 causing 1 death in 8. All these estimates, so far as they can be relied upon—and they undoubtedly approximate correctness—show a smaller proportion of consumption in the United States than exists in England.

No country in the world possesses such a variety of climate and surface as our own, and in none are its inhabitants exposed to greater variations and vicissitudes of temperature: heat and cold, droughts and deluges following each other with alarming rapidity. It is just such a climate and country as this that we are taught to believe is created by nature for the especial development of consumption; yet England, with her more equable climate, presents a higher proportion of deaths from this disease. The only cause that can be assigned for its excess in the latter country is the great humidity of the atmosphere—a fact which might serve to substantiate in some degree the theory of those writers who regard humidity as one of its most prolific causes.

IV.—Statistics of its Prevalence in Various Cities, Regions, and States of the United States.

In examining the statistics of consumption in some of the principal cities of the United States, we find that mere temperature, or the difference of a few degrees in latitude, has very little to do with its prevalence. In New-York city, which has a mean annual temperature of 50°, the proportion of deaths is, as we have seen, 1 in 8.46; while in Charleston, which is situated 8° farther south, and has a mean annual temperature of 64°, 1 to 6.7. The climate, however, is as variable as that of New-York city, and the annual amount of rain about the same. In Philadelphia, with a mean temperature of nearly 54°, the deaths by consumption are 1 in 8.9. In Providence, with a temperature the same as New-York, the proportion is 1 in 6. In Baltimore, with a temperature of 56°, 1 to 6.16. In Chicago, which has a mean temperature of 48°, it is 1 to 10.92. In New-Orleans, the mean temperature of which is 67°, we possess the returns only for the year 1850; the proportion that year was 1 to 11.7. In Memphis, in 1859, it was 1 to 11.3. In Brooklyn, from 1848 to 1859, 1 to 8.11.

In presenting the statistics of consumption in the United States Army, were the proportion of deaths by this disease to that produced by other diseases given, an erroneous idea of its prevalence would be conveyed, as a large part of soldiers attacked by consumption are discharged, to die or recover at home. I have given instead the number in every 1000 men treated for this disease.

Dr. Forrey, in his "Climatology of the United States," shows that the amount of catarrh and influenza in the various posts of the army depends not so much on diurnal variations of temperature as upon the difference of the mean temperature of winter and summer—the amount of these diseases increasing as this difference is greater. Thus, in the posts remote from the ocean and inland seas, this difference is about 56°, and the number of cases per 1000 men treated per annum for these diseases is 552; at the posts on the New-England coast, where the difference is 38°, the number of cases of catarrh and influenza is 233 per 1000 men; while at the posts on the peninsula of Florida, which have but a variation of about 11° between the mean temperature of winter and summer, only 143 cases per 1000 men occur. The same proportion between the amount of the above-mentioned diseases and the variation in temperature exists at the other posts.

Catarrhal diseases and phthisis pulmonalis are frequently supposed to go hand in hand; but, contrary to the opinions often entertained on this point, those conditions of climate which are most productive of such affections of the air-passages as catarrh and influenza do not seem to be most favorable to the development of consumption. The latter disease, indeed, so far from being connected with, seems often quite independent of the causes which produce the former. Thus, we find that while, at the posts on the New-England coast, the difference between the mean temperature of winter and summer is 38°, at the posts on the northern chain of lakes it is 43°; at the posts on the Lower Mississippi 24°; and in the peninsula of East Florida 11°. And there is a proportionate difference in the amount of catarrhal diseases: there being treated annually, in the first of these series, 233 cases among each 1000 men; 300 per 1000 in the second series; 218 in the third, and only 143 in the fourth, the number of cases of consumption treated at *each* of the series is the same—namely, 9 in every 1000 men; and at the posts remote from the ocean and inland seas, where the difference in temperature and the amount of catarrhal diseases is much greater than at any of the other series, the amount of consumption is much less—there being but 5 cases per 1000 men. On the contrary, we find that the greatest number of cases—namely, 13 per 1000 men—is treated on the stations on the coast, from Delaware Bay to Savannah; and the next greatest, 11 per 1000, at the stations in the south-western part of the United States, the difference in the temperature of winter and summer being about 34°, or 11° less than in the northern, and 17° greater than in the southern stations. I shall have occasion to refer again to the comparative prevalence of catarrhal diseases and consumption.

In the Medical Reports of our Army the whole of the United States is divided into about twenty-four departments, the military posts in each being from two to twelve in number, and located in almost every variety of climate and situation. I have endeavored to group together the various series of posts with reference to the amount of consumption in each, and to certain climatic characteristics possessed in common.

These reports show that the greatest number of cases among our troops occurs at the stations situated on the Atlantic coast, between 30° and 35° of north latitude—including the city of Charleston—at the posts in Georgia, Louisiana, Mississippi, and Alabama, situated on or near the Gulf of Mexico, and including the city of New-Orleans, and the posts on the Gulf coast of Florida—the number of cases treated annually being, in the first series of stations, 9.2; in the second, 7.2; and, in the third, 6.9 per 1000 men. The climate of each of these series is characterized by a very high temperature—the average annual temperature being about 80°—abundant rains, and excessive moisture.

The series of posts where, next to those mentioned above, it prevails most extensively, are those of the Harbor of New-York, of North and South California, and those of the department between the eastern slope of the Alleghanies and the Mississippi, and 36° and 40° of north latitude,—the ratio of cases per 1000 men being respectively, 5.9, 5.6, and 5.2.

These posts have many characteristics in common: situated between 32° and 40° of latitude, they have a mean annual temperature of from 50° to 56°, a moderate amount of rain, and are alike subject to great diurnal variations of temperature. There is very much less rain in California than in New-York, though the atmosphere is quite moist, and the climate is milder and much more equable—the difference, in South California, between the mean temperature of winter and summer being only 7°.

The stations on the coast of New-England, between the great lakes and the Atlantic Ocean—so far from each other as to be influenced by neither of these bodies of water, those situated on the great lakes, and those between the great lakes and the Rocky Mountains, are all north of 40° latitude, have only a moderate amount of rain, less than the preceding class of stations, some of them a very high elevation, are exposed to great variations of temperature, are cold and comparatively dry, and have a low temperature—from 38° to 45°. These stations present the next largest proportion of cases of consumption—namely, from 4.1 to 4.8 per 1000 men, the smallest number occurring at the posts which have the highest elevation and the smallest amount of rain.

We find the next smallest proportion of cases—3.8 per 1000 men—in Southern and Western Texas, the stations of which are situated in latitude from 25° to 33° north, having a warm climate, the average annual temperature being about 68°, a moderate amount of rain, and rather a dry atmosphere. Many of these stations have a high elevation, and most of them are subject to great and sudden changes of temperature.

In the departments which have a cold equable climate, a high elevation, and a large amount of rain—

namely those in Washington and Oregon Territories—3.2 cases per 1000 are treated. 2.4 per 1000 occur in the posts which have a moderate amount of rain, a moderate temperature, between 51° and 56°; these posts are situated on the Atlantic coast, between 35° and 40° latitude, and between the Atlantic slope and the Mississippi, and 39° and 40° of latitude. 2.3 cases occur in those stations which have a high temperature, the average annual temperature being 73°, the diurnal variations of which, as well as the difference between the temperature of winter and summer, are slight, a small amount of rain, and a moist salt air. These stations include those on the Atlantic coast of Florida. Only 2 cases per 1000 men occur in those stations which have a high temperature, a dry climate with only a moderate amount of rain and moisture: these stations being situated between 34° and 35° north latitude in the Indian Territory.

Probably the smallest proportion of cases of consumption which exists in the United States—viz., 1.3 in every 1000 men—is found in New-Mexico, a country which has a high elevation—from 3,000 to 8,000 feet—a moderate temperature, and an atmosphere altogether remarkable for its extreme dryness. The annual amount of rain at the various stations is from 11 to 19 inches. So great is the rarity and dryness of the atmosphere that sensible perspiration is almost unknown, even under the severest physical exertion, and caravans cure their beef without salt by hanging slices from their wagon-boxes till it is sufficiently dried. A writer, speaking of the prevalence of consumption here, says: "I have seen but two cases, and each was developed before leaving the United States."

Thus we find, in the examinations of the returns of all these stations, that the amount of consumption is greatest where there is the highest temperature and the greatest amount of rain; next, in the stations which have a moderate temperature and a moderate amount of rain, but the climates of which are moist and characterized by great variations in the diurnal temperature; third, in the stations with rather a low temperature, a moderate amount of rain, and a somewhat drier climate than the preceding class; fourth, at the posts which have a high temperature, a mild dry climate, generally a high elevation, but subject to great variations of temperature; fifth, in those which have a cold equable climate, a high elevation, and a large amount of rain; sixth, in those which have a high temperature, a moist salt air, and very equable climate; seventh, in the stations with a high temperature, a dry climate with a moderate amount of rain and moisture, and last and least in those which have a high elevation, a moderate temperature, and a dry atmosphere.

The following table, constructed from the mortality reports of the United States census of 1850, is presented, not because it can be considered as giving a correct statement of the real amount of consumption, but because it is of value in representing the *relative* amount in the different States. Certain disproportions in the amount of the disease in some of the States can be accounted for only upon the supposition that there are important errors in the returns, which would, of course, impair the value of the whole, except so far as they served to afford an approximate idea of the prevalence of the disease. The table will, however, be found to show an amount of consumption in some of the States agreeing very nearly with the proportion shown to exist when giving the statistics of the United States Army.

It is to be hoped that, ere long, our national government will bestow the attention which the importance of the subject demands upon the registration of deaths throughout the United States, and that we shall have returns of mortality throughout the country equal in accuracy to those which are made in England and throughout the Continent. Obviously such returns, from a country so vast and varied as ours, would be of the greatest value in determining many points in regard to the influence exerted by climate upon certain diseases.*

Proportion of Deaths from Consumption in the various States and Territories of the Union in the year 1850.

STATES.	DEATHS BY CONSUMPTION.
Alabama	1 in 25.8
Arkansas	1 .. 22.8
California[1]	1 .. 100.5
Columbia, District of	1 .. 6.2
Connecticut	1 .. 5.9
Delaware	1 .. 10.2
Florida	1 .. 21.6
Georgia	1 .. 35.5
Illinois	1 .. 13.5
Indiana	1 .. 11.8
Iowa	1 .. 12.8
Kentucky	1 .. 11.6
Louisiana	1 .. 18.6
Maine	1 .. 4.4

* Since the above was written the American Association for the Advancement of Science, at their meeting held the past summer at Newport, have taken measures, by the appointment of a committee for the purpose of arranging a complete system of registration, to remedy the imperfect system which at present exists.

STATES.	DEATHS BY CONSUMPTION.
Maryland	1 in 8.7
Massachusetts	1 .. 5.6
Michigan	1 .. 6.8
Minnesota[2]	1 .. 29.0
Mississippi	1 .. 26.1
Missouri	1 .. 18.8
New-Hampshire	1 .. 4.5
New-Jersey	1 .. 7.0
New-Mexico[3]	1 .. 72.3
New-York	1 .. 6.8
North Carolina	1 .. 18.0
Ohio	1 .. 11.3
Oregon	1 .. 9.4
Pennsylvania	1 .. 8.1
Rhode Island	1 .. 4.7
South Carolina	1 .. 30.1
Tennessee	1 .. 13.5
Texas	1 .. 27.2
Utah	1 .. 20.6
Virginia	1 .. 11.7
Vermont[4]	1 .. 4.1
Wisconsin	1 .. 10.0

[1] The very small proportion of deaths from consumption this year, in this State, is undoubtedly connected with the circumstance that the population whence the returns were derived—being made up to a great extent, in 1850, of emigrants drawn thither by the gold mania, which prevailed so extensively at this time, from various parts of the Union, most of whom were over twenty-five years of age—was, as a whole, much older than the population

of the other States. The whole number of deaths reported this year was 905, of which 9 were by consumption.

[2] Whole number of deaths 29; by consumption 1. Data too small to form the basis of any conclusions.

[3] Whole number of deaths 1157; from consumption, 16. These figures are probably a correct representation of the amount of consumption which exists in this State—the smallest, it may be seen, of any except California.

[4] The census returns of this State for the years 1857 and 1858 showed a similar fearful mortality from this disease: the proportion of deaths being 1 in 4.5.

It may thus be seen—and the conclusion is supported by other returns—that the ravages of consumption are far more extensive in the New-England States than in any other part of the Union.

V.—Rarity and Absence of Consumption in Certain Climates and Countries.

There are some regions of the globe which enjoy a complete immunity from consumption; such regions are generally situated in a high latitude, and, indeed, we find, in proportion to the intensity and long continuance of the cold, a proportionate decrease in the amount of consumption. In Iceland, from 1827 to 1837, there was not a single case, and, according to a writer who has made the diseases of that country his study, it is entirely unknown. I am also informed, by those who have passed a long time in those regions, that in Greenland and Labrador they had never known among the Esquimaux a single case of consumption, and that catarrhal and bronchial affections are almost never met with.* It seems also to be a very rare

* It may be interesting to state here, that similar statements with regard to the absence of catarrhal affections in cold regions have been made by various writers and voyagers, Sir E. Parry amongst them.

We are not, however, to attribute entirely to the influence exerted by the climate, the immunity from consumption enjoyed disease in upper Russia, and in Western Siberia, and seldom exists in the Steppes of the Kirghis—the vast tract of Central Asia between 44° and 55° of north latitude, consisting chiefly of barren plains which abound in salt lakes. The disease is also unknown in Finmarck. In Alexandria, situated in 31° of latitude, with an atmosphere saturated with saline vapor, consumption is almost wholly unknown; and in Teheran, Persia, situated in north latitude 35°, with an elevated position, and rarified air, it is very rare. In Beyrout, Syria, on the Mediterranean, in latitude 33° north, and with a moderate amount of rain, of 4,298 cases, treated at the English Dispensary in 1843, there were but 5 of consumption. In Algiers, situated between 35° and 37° north latitude, with a moderate temperature, there were in 1839, '40, and '41, out of 6,678 deaths, 234 by consumption, or 1 in 28. In 1852–3 the deaths by consumption were 1 in 14.1—an amount nearly double that which prevailed eleven years before, but in each series a very small proportion.

---

by the inhabitants of these regions, but partly to their diet, which consists almost exclusively of fat and animal oils, these affording to the system that supply of nourishment which, from the very commencement of the disease, the weakened and deranged organs of nutrition refuse to yield.

VI.—Statistics of its Prevalence in Various Cities, Countries, and Climates throughout the Globe.

The medical statistics of the British Army, extending as they do over a considerable number of years, and derived from large bodies of men, afford us much valuable information in regard to the prevalence of consumption, as well as of diseases of the lungs generally, in different parts of the world, and serve to give a correct impression in regard to the influence of certain varieties of climate upon the disease.

Thus we find that, in the United Kingdom, out of 44,611 troops, 5.5 men per 1000 were attacked by consumption. In the West India Islands—or that part of them designated as the Windward and Leeward Command, situated between 10° and 19° north latitude—during the same period, out of 86,661 troops, 1023, or 12 per 1000 men were attacked. The amount of all pulmonary diseases in these two climates bear a like proportion to each other: in the former causing 7.7, and in the latter 10.4 deaths in every 1000 men. A great allowance must, however, be made in these comparisons, from the circumstance of the estimate of the two classes of diseases in the United Kingdom, being formed exclusively from the dragoons and dragoon guards, a class of soldiers among whom consumption is hardly half as prevalent as among the foot guards and infantry of the line, while that of the West Indies is formed from the troops indiscriminately. It is evident, however, that consumption is really much more prevalent among the British troops in the West Indies than at home.

These returns show that the views generally entertained with regard to the efficacy of these islands, or of a warm climate by itself, in arresting the development and progress of consumption, are erroneous. The islands of this command, however, present a great variety in their physical configuration and climate, some of them having a moist soil and damp atmosphere, some a dry climate and variable temperature, while others are covered with swamps and marshes. They have an average annual temperature of from 79° to 82°, and but a slight annual variation—4° to 13°.

In two of the stations of the Mediterranean—Gibraltar and Malta, long noted as salutary retreats for the consumptive patient—the disease is actually more prevalent than in Canada, with its long cold winters and great vicissitudes of climate, and, making due allowance for the number of cases sent home, nearly as prevalent as in the United Kingdom.

In Canada, 6.5 men per 1000 are attacked, and 3.8 die of consumption; in Malta, there are 9.8 cases, and 4.3 deaths per 1000 men; and, in Gibraltar, 7 per 1000 are attacked, and 3.62 die—though if in the deaths by this disease in Gibraltar were included the cases which are sent home, the amount would be much larger. Not only, too, are the forces in the Mediterranean better barracked than those in Canada, but nearly half the troops in the latter place (at the time this comparison was made), being under 25 years of age, were much younger as a body than those in the Mediterranean, and so much the more liable therefore to consumption. The amount of diseases of the lungs in general is, however, less than in the United Kingdom and Canada—the proportions being as follows:

	CASES PER 1000 MEN.	DEATHS PER 1000 MEN.
In the United Kingdom....	148	7.7
Canada..................	148	6.7
Gibraltar................	141	5.3
Malta....................	120	6.0

The prevalence of diseases of the lungs in Malta is shown by their having caused, for a period of 13 years, as many as 5.1 deaths in every 1000 of the civil population, or about one less than among the troops; the same ratio within a fraction in which these diseases exist in Sweden; a circumstance which shows conclusively that these complaints may be as prevalent in those countries which have a mild temperature as in those situated in high latitudes and which are subject to cold and great vicissitudes.

In Malta, however, the weather, though often fine, by no means presents that undeviating character so often ascribed to it. The island is rocky and partly undulating, elevated in the centre, and open and exposed on the south and east sides, and, consequently, the coldness and variableness of the weather during the winter and spring are experienced to their full extent. "I have seen," says a writer, "the thermometer stand all day at 32°, with a fresh breeze from the North." In winter and spring fresh breezes from every point of the compass are common, which occasionlly increase to heavy gales. In 1842, 30 per cent., or 1 in 3⅓ of the patients at the Naval Hospital here died of consumption, about the same proportion observed in former years. In Gibraltar, too, according to statistical tables kept for 16 years, east winds prevail 184 days, and west winds 177 days annually. In the winter months the cold is keenly felt.

In the Isle of Mauritius, situated in 20° of south latitude, with a mean temperature of 78°, though with a variable climate, 3.9 men in 1000 (a fraction more than in Canada) die of consumption, or about 1 death in 8.8 is caused by it; while in the Ionian Islands, which are situated between 36° and 40° north latitude, on an average of 20 years, 5 per 1000, or 2 less than in Gibraltar, were attacked, and there was also a smaller proportion of deaths by the disease—3.3 per 1000. The proportion of deaths by all classes of pulmonary diseases is also less, being only 4.8 per 1000, though the climate is more variable, the alternations of temperature more rapid, and the weather more tempestuous than in Gibraltar or Malta.

In the Bermudas, with great uniformity of climate, and a mean temperature of 71° to 75°, 8 per 1000 men were attacked, and 5.1 died. In Newfoundland the deaths were only 4 per 1000; in the Cape of Good Hope, with a mean temperature of 67°, there were 3 deaths per 1000; and in St. Helena, the temperature of which is 61°, about 2—one-ninth part of the total mortality.

While, on the one hand, consumption is rare or

unknown in those countries situated in a high latitude, on the other, we find that it frequently exists in its minimum among the British soldiers stationed in tropical countries. In the Madras Presidency, which is situated between 8° and 20° north latitude, the proportion of deaths by consumption among the British troops has been variously estimated at from .77 to .71 per 1000 men. One writer, however, has placed the proportion of consumption among the English troops in all India as high as 1.9 per 1000 (an estimate probably much too high). Of ten regiments stationed in India generally, during a period of fourteen years, there were but 2.8 cases, and 1.8 deaths by consumption per 1000 men.

Here, however, as in all tropical countries, the progress of the disease is much more rapid than at home: in the British regiments it is said to be chiefly prevalent among two classes of soldiers—youths from the manufacturing towns of England, with constitutions debilitated from labor in the factories, and badly nourished Irishmen, whose systems had become impoverished and deteriorated before enlisting in the army, from insufficient or unwholesome food. According to Boudin, out of 17,420 admissions into the hospitals, there were only 14 deaths by consumption.

In Bengal, which is situated between 20° and 31° of north latitude, M. Collas states that among the Topas, next to cholera, it is the most prevalent of all fatal diseases; except among this class, and the weavers of Cashmere—who are more liable to the disease from the nature of their occupation, which requires a sedentary and stooping position, and is pursued generally in cellars badly ventilated, and the atmosphere of which is filled with particles of floating dust—it is very rare.

Another writer, M. Martin, says, however, that while in England the ratio of cases is about 6.4, and the number of deaths 5.3 per 1000, in Bengal the number of cases is only 1.8 per 1000 men, and the proportion of deaths too small to be calculated.

Ceylon is situated between 5° and 9° of north latitude. It has a hot and moist climate, though the temperature is not so high as on the neighboring continent. The soil is for the most part clayey, and the rains are profuse. Here, consumption is much more prevalent than in India, there being 5.3 attacked, and 3.2 deaths by it per 1000 men; among the Europeans it causes about 1 death in 7.

In Senegal, situated in 10° north latitude, and having the warmest and most variable climate on the globe, it is difficult to estimate the amount of consumption among the troops, so great and rapid is the mortality from diseases peculiar to the climate, but a number of those spared by endemic maladies fall victims to the disease, and a large share of the mortality among the natives is caused by it.

In Sierra Leone, with an annual temperature of 81°, and 189 inches of rain annually, there were, from 1853 to '54, 433 admissions into the hospital, of which only 9 were cases of consumption; and of 113 deaths, it caused only 4. This does not, however, give a correct idea of the liability to the disease in this climate, as the patients, says Dr. Robert Clarke, "are made up from the liberated Africans from the condemned slavers, the colonial poor, and the British and foreign destitute seamen." The black colony here is formed, too, of representatives of almost every tribe of Western Africa. The same writer says that the Negro is extremely liable to phthisis, though he had met with but three cases among Europeans which had originated there.

Madeira, between 32° and 33° of north latitude, with its balmy atmosphere, seldom disturbed by violent winds, and its perpetual summer temperature, the thermometer showing but a variation of 10°

the year round, and having a mean annual temperature of 65°, seems of all countries in the world—unless we except the Hawaiian Islands—best fitted for the mitigation and arrest of consumptive conditions. Patients who come here affected with consumption live three or four years longer than the ordinary duration of the disease in England; and large numbers have resided on the island in perfect health, while their brothers and sisters have fallen victims to the disease at home. With regard to the climate of Madeira, it may be observed that it is between that of the Torrid and Temperate Zones; it is humid, though not foggy. The island itself is rocky and mountainous, and well watered.

If we except the British troops stationed in the Madras Presidency, the forces in New Zealand enjoy a greater immunity from consumption than the troops in any other of the British possessions. The number of deaths here per 1000 men, from all diseases of the lungs, is only 2.4—considerably less than the number of deaths from consumption alone in the Mediterranean stations. These islands are situated between 34° and 37° south latitude, and longitude 166° and 178° east, have a mean annual temperature of 58°, and a moderate amount of rain; the climate is not, however, equable, the temperature ranging throughout the year from 39° to 74°.

In singular contrast to this we find that, in Tahiti and the Marquesas, it is stated to be very common, and to destroy nearly a third of the population. "It occurs much more frequently," says Boudin, "among the women than the men, and, above all, among children. Pulmonary disorganization advances in these countries with frightful rapidity: three or four months are sufficient to bring the sufferer to the grave."—"In a few weeks," says M. Erhel, "they pass from the most flourishing health to the most complete emaciation." Tahiti is situated in 17° south latitude, and longitude 149° west. Its climate, though warm, is not enervating; the most remarkable fact in its medical geography is the complete absence of marsh fevers. "During a sojourn there of three years," says a writer, "I have sought in vain a well-marked case of intermittent fever." In the absence of more minute knowledge of the climate of the island, I am aware of no circumstance to which this alarming prevalence of consumption can be attributed, unless that of the absence of paludal or marsh fevers; the theory, as is well known, having existed, and numbering, among its warmest supporters, many eminent medical writers, that the two cachexiæ, or conditions of the constitution, which are produced by consumption and intermittent fevers are inimical, and cannot exist together; and that the malaria which engenders the latter disease, or frequent attacks of the disease itself, will stop the development or progress of the former affection, and, *mutatis mutandis*, that consumption is most prevalent in countries where intermittent fever is unknown. The correctness of this theory is yet, however, *sub judice.*

In the Hawaiian Islands, on the other hand, we find that, although there are no intermittent fevers, consumption is a very rare disease, almost, indeed, entirely unknown among the foreign and native inhabitants, except among those in whom it has been developed before reaching the islands, and, in the cases of these, being followed by a decided amelioration or a cure.

Chronic bronchitis and catarrhs are, on the contrary, very prevalent. Dr. Gulick, in his essay on the climate and diseases of these islands, speaking of the prayer-meetings held at daybreak, says that, "For the first twenty minutes, it was generally scarcely possible to proceed with the religious exercises, from the incessant coughing of the congregation. It was as though each one was under the necessity of expectorating a certain amount of mucus before respiration could be comfortably carried on." As regards the amount of moisture, the various parts of the islands present a great difference—some being arid, with hardly enough rain to moisten the soil, and some being perpetually moist, the annual amount of rain varying from 25 to 75 inches.

These islands are situated between latitude 18° and 22° north, and between 154° and 160° of west longitude. Their climate, both as regards daily and annual variations, is one of the most equable known—the annual temperature being about 73°; the daily range of thermometer being at Nice 8.5°, at Rome 11°, and at Honolulu 12°; the mean difference of successive months being at St. Augustine (Florida) 3° 68′, at Penzance 3° 05′; at Madeira 2° 41′, and at Honolulu and Waioli about 1° 63′. At St. Augustine the annual range is 53°, at Madeira 23°, and at Honolulu, Lahaina, and Waioli from 24° to 32°. Dr. Judd, in speaking of the evenness of the climate, says that so little is there unusual or noticeable in the weather that the natives seldom speak of it—that there is no word in their language to express that general idea, and it is only the occurrence of a storm or something unusual that attracts sufficient attention to make it a subject of remark.

In London, the mean annual temperature of which is the same as New-York, as we have already seen, consumption causes at present about 1 death in 8.6. In Stuttgart, according to Dr. Caspar, in latitude 48° north, and with a temperature of 49°—1 in 4.7. In Hamburg, with a temperature of 48°, 1 in 4.6; in Amsterdam, with a temperature of 49°, 1 in 4. The mortality from consumption in Paris is about the same as in London. In Berlin, with a temperature of 48°, 1 death in 5.7 is occasioned by it; in Copenhagen, which has a temperature of 46°, a seventh part.

In Russia, in 1855, the deaths in all the civil hospitals were 33,026, of which 3,912, or 1 in 7.8, were by consumption. In the hospital population of Montpelier it causes a third, and of Marseilles and Rouen each, a fourth of the deaths. Havre, situated near the sea, with a free circulation of air, is nearly exempt from the disease.

At Rome 1 death in 40 occurs from consumption; at Naples 1 in 8; at Turin, with a mean annual temperature of 53°, 1 in 3; at Geneva, with a temperature of 75°, 1 in 6; at Nice, 1 in 7.

In the *hospitals* of Florence the deaths from consumption have been variously estimated at from 1 in 6, to 1 in 11.5.

If we compare the mortality from consumption in the hospitals of Naples and Paris, we find it much more prevalent in the former place. From 1835 to '39 the deaths by consumption in the civil hospitals were:

In Naples...........	1 in $2\frac{1}{3}$ of all diseases.
In Paris......... ...	1 " $3\frac{6}{7}$ " "

In the military hospitals, during the same period:

In Naples...................	1 death in $3\frac{6}{7}$
In Paris.....................	1 " $12\frac{1}{5}$

In 1850–51 the deaths by consumption in the French Army of Occupation in Italy were 1 in 6; while in the French Army generally it causes among the infantry but about 1 death in 13.

The Department of Ain is covered with ponds and marshes, and is perhaps in all France the district where intermittent fevers are most prevalent; yet, according to the testimony of several physicians, consumption is almost wholly unknown there. In Venice, with a mean temperature of 57°, and a moist atmosphere, while intermittent fevers prevail extensively, consumption is very rare—among 1200 patients treated at the hospitals there being but 2 cases. In the Tuscan Maremmes, where intermittent fever is abundant, of 81,731 cases of various diseases there were only 100 of consumption, or 1 in 817.

Consumption might be supposed to be rare in Brazil, with its fine climate and uniform temperature; yet we find that, in the maritime cities, a fifth part of the deaths occur from it. At Bahia so great is the rapidity of its progress that it is regarded as an acute disease.

In Constantinople, which has a mean temperature of 56°, and a climate characterized by great variability, consumption is one of the most frequent of diseases, and seems to be as prevalent as in most civilized countries. Something of its prevalence is undoubtedly due to the narrow ill-paved streets, the crowded, dark, and filthy dwellings, and the enervating life of the harem.

In the Canton of Geneva, with a temperature of 49°, and rather a dry climate, the deaths by consumption in 1838 were one-ninth of the whole.

VII.—The Comparative Prevalence of Consumption at Sea and on Land.

The theory has always prevailed, more or less extensively, that the sea may sometimes act, not only as a palliative, but as a preventive of this disease.

There are undoubtedly certain cases and conditions of consumption which may be cured or palliated by sea air, but we must bear in mind the fact that the various stages of a single case of consumption are often quite opposite to each other in their character, so as to make consumption appear as a congeries of distinct diseases, rather than as a single disease, and that, consequently, it would be as irrational to recommend sea air indiscriminately for consumption, as it would a particular medicine.

Were we to form our ideas of the effect of sea air in consumptive conditions from the comparative prevalence of the disease in the army and navy, without taking into consideration certain modifying circumstances which I shall mention, we might, as many others have done, conclude that it is both palliative and preventive. There are many reasons why, aside from the influence of sea voyages, the sailor in the navy should be less liable than the soldier to consumption. Both in the British and the American Navy every means are resorted to, to prevent the admission of men affected with, or in any degree predisposed to phthisis. Recruits for the naval service are subjected to a rigid physical examination before they are received, and the examination is repeated, at the expiration of a few days, when they are admitted to the receiving ship where the recruit is entered, and, finally, when the crew is transferred to a vessel destined for sea service, every man of doubtful efficiency is returned to the receiving ship. Thus every vessel starts upon her voyage with a crew as little liable as possible to a disease of this kind.

Sailors, too, are engaged but for three or four years, at the expiration of which time they are obliged to undergo a physical examination before they can be hired again, a system equivalent to sending home every three or four years all the sailors in the navy not in perfect health, an arrangement which evidently diminishes the ratio of mortality from this disease. In the army, on the contrary, the soldier is hired for a much longer period.

I present, however, the following statistics of the relative prevalence of the disease, without at present considering how much the less frequency of the disease which we generally find to exist among naval than among military forces is owing simply to sea air and to a residence on the sea; though it seems evident that to these are due much of the comparative immunity enjoyed in the navy.

A comparison made in 1842 of the diseases of the naval forces of the East India command of the British Navy, whose operations were confined principally to the Bay of Bengal, the Coromandel or Eastern Coast, and the Island of Ceylon, and the European troops in the Island of Ceylon, gives the following results—results particularly valuable, as the naval and land forces were employed near each other in nearly the same latitude and longitude, were collected during the same period, between 1830 and '37, and from forces whose aggregate strength was nearly the same.

	Aggregate strength.	Whole number attacked by consumption.	Number attacked per 1000 men.	Whole number of deaths by consumption.	Number of deaths per 1000 men.
Naval Forces...	12,942	39	3.0	16	1.2
Military Forces.	14,590	78	5.3	51	3.4

"The less frequency of phthisis in the navy, as shown by this computation," says the authority whence the above facts are derived, "may arise from the frequent change of station in the navy, from the shorter exposure to the debilitating influences of a tropical climate, and from the less prevalence of fever, which is undoubtedly a frequent exciting cause in persons predisposed to phthisis." Another reason is doubtless that the period of a sailor's stay in these regions rarely exceeds four years, while the term of service of a regiment in Ceylon is ten years, and the longer they remain the less power of resistance have their constitutions to disease.

Diseases of the lungs generally, and catarrhal affections particularly, were, however, much more prevalent in the navy than in the army; thus, out of the forces above mentioned, the proportions were as follows:

	Aggregate strength.	Total number attacked.	Number attacked per 1000 men.	Total number of deaths.	Number of deaths per 1000 men.
Naval Forces...	12,942	2,501	193	24	1.8
Land Forces....	14,590	1,158	79	83	5.6

Thus we see that these diseases are accompanied by a much greater mortality in the army than in the navy; in the former, inflammation of the lungs and phthisis predominating, in the latter, catarrhal affections, the sailor being much more liable to these complaints from the circumstances that he is more exposed to the vicissitudes of the weather, is obliged to turn out every night from his close, over-heated berth to take his turn on deck, and from his being allowed to wear whatever clothing he pleases, while the soldier is obliged to wear his greatcoat at night.

These statistics confirm the opinion given, when speaking of the relative amount of consumption and catarrhal affections in the United States Army, that there is no necessary connection between the two diseases, and that they usually exist quite independently of each other.*

A comparison instituted between the naval and land forces serving in the Mediterranean stations from 1830 to 1843 gives the following results:

	Aggregate strength.	Number of men per 1000 attacked by consumption.	Number of deaths per 1000 men by consumption.
Naval Forces...	102,464	4.5	1.7
Land Forces....	102,214	6.1	4.0

In the naval forces there were 251 cases and 3.1 deaths, and in the land forces 144 cases and 5.9 deaths per 1000 men from diseases of the lungs, the proportion approximating that obtained from the comparison presented of the amount of these diseases among the soldiers and sailors of the East India command.

In 1856 there were attacked, in the whole of the British Navy, 5.6 men per 1000, while the deaths per 1000 were 2.7.

* These affections, however, frequently act as exciting causes of consumption.

In the squadron stationed in the East Indies and China coast from 1837 to 1843, in the Mediterranean Squadron, the Home Squadron, and .the irregular naval forces from 1830 to 1836, there were attacked per 1000 men, by consumption, 7.6. This large proportion of consumptive cases can hardly be considered a fair estimate of its prevalence in the navy generally, as there enter into the data from which the estimate is drawn, the returns of one of the squadrons in which the disease is most prevalent of any in the navy—viz., the Home Squadron, many of the vessels of which remain in one port a whole year, the sailors being permitted to pass a great deal of time on shore, while no returns from the squadrons in which the disease exists in its minimum, are included.

Thus we find, accepting this last large estimate, from the statistics given above, that there were attacked in the British Navy 5 men per 1000. In the whole British Army the number attacked per 1000 is about 6.6.

In our own navy, from 1855 to 1860, out of an aggregate force of 29,258 men, there were attacked per 1000 by consumption, 4.3. In our army about 4.2 men are attacked per 1000.

These last figures, however, are deduced from

medical reports of the army and navy made at different periods, those of the former extending from 1840 to 1855, and those of the latter from 1855 to 1860. A comparison made from returns derived from similar periods might give a different result.

The prevalence of the disease varies very much in the different squadrons, there being attacked per 1000 men, in the—

Brazil Squadron	2.3
Home "	2.9
African "	4.4
Mediterranean Squadron	4.7
East India "	5.0
Pacific "	6.1

The mortality from consumption in the navy is certainly very small. Owing, however, to the facilities which exist in the navy for sending home invalids, we must not conclude that its mortality is proportionate to the ratio of its prevalence.

From 1830 to 1836 the effective total of the British Navy was 157,770 sailors. The total number of deaths by consumption during this period was 166, or 1.7 per 1000 men, the mortality among the various squadrons being as follows:

the Home Squadron, the Squadrons stationed on the West Coast of Africa, the Cape of Good Hope, and South America, each 1.7 per 1000 men; the Squadrons of the West Indies and North America, of the Mediterranean, Peninsular Spain, and Portugal, each 1.9; of the East Indies, 1.4.

The returns of the different squadrons from 1837 to 1843, show the mortality from consumption to have been 1.5 per 1000.

In the British Army the number of deaths per 1000 men by consumption is about 4.09.

In our own navy, from 1855 to 1860, out of an aggregate force of 29,258 men, only 7, or 0.2 per 1000 died of consumption.

In our army, from 1840 to 1855, there died by consumption 2.4 per 1000 men.

There are no means of ascertaining the prevalence of the disease in our mercantile marine; it is, however, of frequent occurrence among the Nantucket whalers.

VIII.—The Mortality from Consumption at Different Months and Seasons of the Year.

It would be of more practical use were we able to tell the number of cases of consumption *developed*, than the number that die from the disease in the different months of the year. The former, of course, we cannot know. In every month it is fearfully fatal. Dr. Caspar, from tables of 11,472 cases, carefully kept at Berlin during a period of nine years, shows that the mortality of various winters bears no connection with the difference of temperature. In the coldest of the nine winters, which had an average temperature of 24°, there were 393 deaths from consumption; and in the warmest, with a temperature of 36°, the number was nearly the same. The temperature of three winters was almost the same—32° and 33°, yet there was a great variation in the number of deaths—there being in one 345, in another 284. The average temperature of the warmest spring was 50°, and the mortality was as much above the average as in the coldest, which had a temperature of less than 44°. Dr. Caspar also shows by these tables that the difference in the mortality was very slight in the winters in which the variations in temperature were greatest, while it was very strongly marked in the winters in which the variations were very slight. So far as any deductions could be drawn, the mortality was least, those winters in which the barometer was highest—the average height of the barometer during this period being 29.79 inches.

Dr. Caspar is of the opinion that the changes in dress, the difference in diet, in the amount of time passed in and out of doors, and of habits generally, in the various seasons, have a greater influence in determining the mortality from consumption than the difference in the atmospherical conditions.

In a table which I have constructed, of 212,407 deaths from consumption, occurring in various years, at New-York, Philadelphia, Paris, Providence, Baltimore, Boston, Chicago, London, and New-Orleans, I find that the mortality of the different months, commencing with that in which it is highest, is as follows:

March	21,950
April	20,897
May	19,971

February	18,663
January	18,600
December	18,046
June	17,523
July	16,523
November	16,360
August	16,087
September	15,387
October	14,209

Arranged according to the seasons, the deaths were, in the—

Spring	61,945
Winter	55,309
Summer	50,197
Autumn	45,956

A table of 12,668 deaths occurring from consumption, in Paris, Milan, and other cities of Europe, shows a corresponding rate of mortality in the different seasons; there being, in the—

Spring	3,482	deaths.
Winter	3,109	"
Summer	3,076	"
Autumn	3,001	"

IX.—Comparative Prevalence of Consumption in the City and Country.

So far as the statistics which we have at hand enable us to judge, consumption does not seem necessarily more prevalent in large than in small cities. It is, however, somewhat less prevalent in all the rural districts of England, than in London. During a period of six months, in 1837, in which the deaths from consumption in the rural districts were 3.5 per 1000, they were 4 per 1000 in London, 4.8 in Birmingham and Leeds, and 6.4 in Liverpool; though, while it caused in all England, except London, 1 death in 5, in London it caused but 1 in 6.

There are, however, but few towns in the rural districts of England so free from consumption as London. In Devonshire, during the same period, one-fifth, and, in Norfolk and Suffolk, one-fourth of the entire mortality was due to this disease. During a later period, from 1847 to 1857, while in all England it caused 1 death in 8, in London it caused but 1 in 8.6.

It was observed, in the Hôpital Cochin, that in cases in which the disease was hereditary, no immunity was enjoyed from the circumstance of the patients being born of parents who were natives of the country, or who had themselves been raised in the country.

A French writer, M. Fourcault, assumes the mortality to be much less in small towns and villages which do not contain more than 2,000 inhabitants, and which have an elevated situation. Under these favorable circumstances, he asserts that not more than one-fortieth of the entire mortality is owing to it, and, in villages still less densely populated, not more than one-sixtieth or one-hundredth part. The small amount of consumption under these circumstances is, however, undoubtedly due as much to the elevated situation as to the mere thinness of population; nor, indeed, so much depends on the circumstances of soil, climate, and situation, is any general affirmation that consumption is either more or less prevalent in the country than in the city, admissible.

X.—Influence of Light and Darkness upon its Existence.

How much influence is exerted upon the prevalence of consumption by light and darkness? two agents which exercise such a controlling influence upon health and upon animal and vegetable life. From the deterioration in the activity of the animal functions which accompanies a long deprivation of light, it might be supposed, *à priori*, that consumption would be much more likely to exist under circumstances in which the darkness was of long continuance. The elaborate work of M. Boudin on medical geography and statistics affords us much useful information on this point, and I cannot do better than to present entire a literal translation of his interesting remarks:

"Past the Polar circle," he says, "a continued day follows a long night, and the absence of an alternation of light and darkness exercises a marked influence for the worse, upon the health. Sleep, particularly, is neither complete nor restorative. In winter the inhabitants of the smaller cities try, by dancing and acting comedies, to lengthen out the evening to the latest possible moment; for every one, knowing that he will not obtain the sleep which he desires, defers as long as possible the hour of retiring. Above all are the women and children affected by this insomnia; even the infants toss restlessly throughout the whole night in their cradles; soon they become pale and rachitic, and die if they are not sent to a better climate—to the south of Norway. The same inconvenience, as we know by personal experience, and the experience of the natives of the country has been the same, exists in summer. The sun does not set, the stimulating action of the light is unceasing, and the need of sleep is not felt as with us. At eleven o'clock, at midnight, and even at one o'clock, the inhabitants are to be found in the streets, or standing idly before their doors; and when, finally, overcome by a feeling of fatigue and lassitude, repose is sought, it is to find only a restless sleep which proves but slightly invigorating. It is of but little use to create artificial darkness, as the inhabitants seem to have discovered, for their windows are supplied with neither shutters nor blinds.

"These influences leave their impress upon the

physical constitution of the inhabitants of Finmarck. The males, and especially the females, are slender, blanched, and often rachitic; spinal incurvations are frequent, menstruation difficult and tardy, *embonpoint* is rare, and the cheeks seldom have any color. In the midst of all these physiological and physical circumstances," says M. Martins, "one would suppose that consumption would be very common; notwithstanding, I believe it to be very rare, and I do not remember ever to have seen a single consumptive patient in Finmarck, and all the physicians of Scandinavia are of the opinion that the disease becomes less frequent as we advance farther towards the North."—*Traité de Géographie et de Statistique Médicales.* Vol. II., page 630.

XI.—Its Prevalence among Different Races.

There is no reason for supposing that, in his native land, and surrounded by those climatic influences under which nature intended him to reside, the Negro is more liable than the white man to consumption. I have excellent authority for stating that the disease is rare amongst the Negroes in Africa, and in the interior is almost never known. But it is found that, as the Negro is removed from his native clime, his predisposition to the disease increases. Thus in all the stations (with the single exception of the Madras Presidency) in which Negro and European troops have been quartered together, the former have been the greater sufferers, not only from consumption, but from diseases of the lungs generally. It may here be stated that, of all the deaths from diseases of the lungs in the British Army, about four-fifths are estimated to be caused by consumption.

From 1817 to 1839 the annual losses per 1000

men, from these diseases, among the native or black, and the European troops, were as follows:

	EUROPEANS.	NEGROES.
Windward and Leeward Islands	10.4	16.5
Jamaica....................	7.5	10.3
Mauritius...........	5.6	12.9
Sierra Leone................	4.9	6.3
Cape of Good Hope, Eastern Frontier................	2.4	3.9
Madras Presidency...........	2.3	0.7

This predisposition, under the above-mentioned circumstances, of Negroes to diseases of the chest, is rendered more apparent by a comparison of the mortality from these diseases with that among other troops than of European origin.

In the Isle of Ceylon, where there were bodies of soldiers from five different provinces, the mortality was as follows. Among the—

	DEATHS PER 1000 MEN.
Native Troops.........................	1.6
Troops recruited from India............	1.9
Pioneers (same origin)................	2.5
Malays.............................	3.6
English Troops.......................	4.1
Black Troops (Negro)................	10.5

As regards the comparative amount of consumption in particular, we find the deaths per 1000 men from this affection, during a period of from 19 to 20 years, on the—

	NEGROES.	WHITES.
West Coast of Africa........	4.0	?
Honduras..................	6.6	?
Bahamas....................	7.0	?
Jamaica.....................	7.5	7.4
Mauritius....................	6.4	3.9
Antilles......................	9.8	6.4
Gibraltar....................	33.5	6.1

At the Cape of Good Hope, the deaths from consumption among the Hottentots and British soldiers are about the same: 2.4 per 1000.

In New-York city, during 1856 and '57, while it caused, of the deaths among the white population, 1 in 8.6, among the black population, during the same period, it caused 1 in 4.37.

In Charleston, from 1822 to 1849, the proportion of deaths from this disease among the whites and blacks was nearly the same: 15.20 per cent. of the white population during that period, and 14.46 per cent. of the black, falling victims to it; the excess being a little among the whites. The liability to consumption in this climate is, however, stated by the census report of Charleston, to be about the same in the two races.

In Egypt, consumption is very rare among the Turks, Armenians, Jews, Copts, and Europeans; though, when once declared, it progresses rapidly. The Negroes and Abyssinians are, on the contrary, decimated by it. "Egypt," says an English writer, "seems to be the northern climate of the black races; nor can the great prevalence of consumption amongst them be attributed to the privations and hardships of slavery, as they are much better cared for and fed than most of the poor classes of the population."

In Algiers, during the years 1839, '40, and '41, the total number of deaths was 6,678, of which 234 were by consumption. We find a vast disproportion in the mortality it occasioned among the Europeans, Moors, and Jews: among the first causing 1 death in 9.3, among the second 1 in 40.7, and among the last 1 in 36.9.

XII.—Its Prevalence among the Various Trades and Professions.

If we except the relative amount of consumption in different climates, we find the difference in its prevalence nowhere so strongly marked as among the various trades and professions. In a table constructed by M. de Neufville, based on eight years' observations at Frankfort on the Main, of 100 deaths, occurring among each of these callings, there were, among—

Tailors	39.9	deaths.
Shoemakers	38.4	"
Painters	32.9	"
Locksmiths and Blacksmiths	30.9	"
Professors	29.7	"
Gardeners	28.7	"
Brewers	26.3	"
Carpenters	25 9	"
Bakers	23.3	"
Merchants	22.9	"
Physicians and Surgeons	18.2	"
Masons	17.1	"
Butchers	8.2	"
Lawyers and Magistrates	6.8	"

The maximum of deaths from the disease being among the tailors, and the minimum among the lawyers, and next among butchers. It is to be regretted that no statement of the proportion of deaths among farmers is given in the above table.

It has been computed that, in London, a fourth part of the bakers have consumptive symptoms.

There seems to be, sometimes, a curious exemption among tobacco workers. Several years ago it was ascertained that, among the 5,000 workmen employed by the Government in the tobacco manufactories of France, though they were often ill with catarrh, consumption was much less prevalent than among the inhabitants of the districts in which they dwelt. At Bordeaux it was not only rare among the workmen, but its progress was slow; at Havre no cases had been observed; nor had any cases been known to exist among the workmen at Strasbourg, though their families were subject to it; and at Marlaix and Lille it was much less common than among other workmen. They were not subject to epidemics, typhoid fevers, nor influenza. The only explanation that I am aware of, of this immunity enjoyed by tobacco workers, is that of M. Simon, who attributes it to the narcotic properties of the tobacco.

It is stated, in the Report of the Registrar-General of England, that, in the year 1851, the deaths between the ages of 35 and 45 were, among farmers, 9 per 1000; among carpenters, 10 per 1000; among shoemakers, 11; among blacksmiths, 12; among tailors, 14; among bakers, 15; and among butchers, 17. Between the ages of 45 and 55, the mortality among butchers was 23, and between the ages of 55 and 65, 41 per 1000—a much higher rate of mortality than prevailed among any of the other classes above mentioned.

The fact that there is a smaller rate of mortality amongst these classes past the age of 35 years than among butchers, may perhaps find its explanation in the circumstance that it is among these very classes that consumption is most prevalent, and, as the most frequent and fatal period of consumption is between the ages of 20 and 35 years, their mortality must be greatest previous to their thirty-fifth year, and proportionately less after it. Butchers, on the contrary, not being particularly subject to any fatal disease, find their greatest period of mortality as they advance farther on in life.

Dr. Guy states that, in London, the proportion of consumptive cases among gentry and professional men is 16 per cent.; among tradesmen 28, and among all kinds of laboring men, 30 per cent.

He assigns, as the cause of this great prevalence among tradesmen, the fact that they are confined so many hours within doors, occupying a middle place between in and out-door laborers and men following sedentary in-door pursuits. According to the same writer the amount of consumption among men working in-doors and those working out-doors is as 1 to 3.81 in the former, and 1 to 4.13 in the latter. As regards the amount of consumption among men working in-doors, and using different degrees of exertion, the ratio among those following sedentary pursuits is 1 to 3.08; among those using more exertion, 1 to 4.44, and among those whose occupations demand great exertion, 1 to 5.06. Among single females, leading sedentary lives, there were three times as many cases of consumption as amongst those taking active exercise, as servants, housekeepers, and shopwomen. Among females generally, the smallest amount of consumption was amongst those employed out of doors.

Dr. Guy also found that, in a large printing establishment, the deaths from consumption among compositors, who were obliged to occupy an unvarying and constrained position, amounted to 74 per cent.; among the pressmen, whose labors required the exercise of the whole body, only 31; and, among those of the operatives who took regular exercise in the open air, only 25 per cent. He does not, however, attribute this vast disproportion solely to the difference in the amount of exercise; but, in part, to the fact that the compositor often selects his particular department from the circumstance of not being sufficiently robust to perform heavy presswork. He considers the exercise chiefly of value in assisting to get rid of the effects of impure air, which effects are increased by comparative inaction; instancing, in support of this opinion, the good health and long lives enjoyed by literary men, who lead sedentary lives, but enjoy an abundance of pure air. Dr. Guy seems disinclined to give exercise, in this case, its due credit; many literary men, including the most indefatigable workers, passing but a small portion of their time at their labors, and a good deal in the open air.

His final conclusions are, that the ratio of cases of consumption to those of all other diseases, is highest, when the amount of exertion is least, and lowest, when greatest; an intermediate amount of exertion presenting an intermediate ratio.

Sir James Clarke divides the callings by which the prevalence of consumption is influenced, into two classes: those which act as local irritants of the lungs, and those which exercise an injurious effect upon the whole economy. Among the former, he places the trade of the mason, the grinder, and the flax-dresser. To the second, those agencies belong which affect the general health and induce tuberculous cachexiæ; such, for example, as do not afford sufficient bodily exerise, and are attended with a deficiency of pure air. To their passing so much time in the open air he ascribes the comparative immunity from this disease enjoyed by butchers and tanners.

XIII.—Consumption among the Rich and Poor.

It was estimated by M. Lombard that consumption is twice as prevalent among the bulk of the population as among that part of it situated in easy circumstances. According to a statistical account published by M. Espine, the mortality from consumption amounted to 68 per 1000 among those in rich and easy circumstances; 155 per 1000 among the general population; while among the poor the proportion was 233 per 1000. These statistics were, however, drawn more particularly from the city of Geneva. The causes of this predominance of the disease among the poor, are to be found in their insufficient or improper food, their badly-ventilated dwellings, and their want of personal cleanliness; but perhaps, above all, in the mental depression and listlessness so frequently attendant upon conditions of life whose daily provisions are fraught with anxiety and discontent—the influence of the mind upon the status of the body being too well known to need any comment. A French physician, M. Elie, once stated that four-fifths of mankind die of grief! Nor, though it may seem at first even laughable, is this assertion without some claim to respect. He does not mean to have us infer that men die directly of broken hearts, or that a reverse in business will necessarily prostrate the vital forces beyond that point whence there is no recalling them; but he does mean that they may die of diseases, whether they come in the shape of brain or nervous fever or dyspepsia, springing from exhausted and irritated conditions of the nervous system, which, in turn, has become disordered by prolonged and harassing conditions of the mind. In no disease does the mind exercise a more direct influence upon the physical condition, than in consumption. In despondency and grief, the respirations are longer and less frequent; the lungs, the favorite seat of tubercular disease, are in a semi-congested state, the blood does not enter and leave them with its usual readiness, and a condition exists calculated to invite congestions, while that prostration of the nervons strength which is often the earliest and most frequent symptom in this disease, is easily induced. In short, the nerve force—which regulates the whole economy, and particularly that which presides over the proper nutrition of the system, and upon the derangement of which, consumption may be regarded as dependent—is paralyzed.

XIV.—Its Prevalence in Manufacturing Towns.

So far as we can derive any information from the statistics of Manchester and Belfast, consumption does not seem more prevalent among the operatives in cotton and linen factories than among other classes of operatives.

A number of years ago, Mr. Noble, an English surgeon, presented a number of statistics by which he showed that the proportion of deaths by consumption in Manchester did not exceed that of other English towns—that they did not occur more frequently, nor at an earlier age among the operatives in the factories than among the other inhabitants of the town; but, on the contrary, the ratio of the mortality was less than in various other cities and the surrounding agricultural districts.

During a period in which the deaths from consumption in this city amounted to 15¾ per cent. of the whole, in Essex, one of the most purely agricultural districts in England, while the general mortality was much less than in Manchester, that from consumption amounted to 19 per cent. A similar result followed a comparison with other agricultural districts of England—Cambridgeshire, Huntingtonshire, and Lincolnshire—in which, while the relative mortality was less, the per-centage of deaths from consumption was greater than in Manchester, being 18 per cent. of the whole. Nor did a comparison with several cities show that Manchester enjoyed a relative immunity from consumption when contrasted simply with agricultural districts. In Liverpool and West Derby, the deaths from consumption were 20 per cent., and in Birmingham, a city also exempt from factory labor, 18 per cent. The proportion of consumptive cases in London, at about the same time, was smaller in comparison with its size than in any other English city, being only 15¾ per cent.

Nor was an undue proportion of the consumptive cases of Manchester furnished from the factory population. The total number of deaths from consumption, during the period referred to, was 1141, of which 174, or about one-sixth, occurred among the operatives. As this class formed about a sixth part of the entire population, the ratio of deaths from the disease, among the operatives and the other inhabitants of the town, was, therefore, about the same.

That factory labor does not induce consumption at an earlier age than do other occupations, is demonstrated by various facts—such as the following:

The 174 deaths above referred to as occurring among the operatives, were mostly between the ages of 15 and 40—the period of life at which consumption is most liable to occur under ordinary circumstances. The whole 1141 deaths from consumption were divided among the different periods of life as follows:

AGES.	NUMBER OF DEATHS.
15 to 20 years	195
20 " 25 "	243
25 " 30 "	260
30 " 35 "	223
35 " 40 "	220
Total	1141

A table which does not show a greater mortality during the earlier periods of life than we should ordinarily expect.

Sir James Clarke constructed a table of 1000 deaths from consumption, deduced from observations made promiscuously in Edinburgh, Berlin, Nottingham, Philadelphia, Chester, Carlisle, and Paris. By including certain tables referring only to Carlisle and Paris and to Manchester, we find a total of 1155 deaths for the two former places, and of 1141 for the latter—the numbers at various ages, of the respective series being as follows:

AGES.	CARLISLE AND PARIS.	MANCHESTER.
Between 15 and 20 years	196	195
" 20 " 30 "	515	503
" 30 " 40 "	444	443
Total....................	1155	1141

"A most remarkable accordance," says the author, "in the ages of persons dying of consumption under very different external circumstances."

We are, however, by no means to regard these data, taken as they are from one town alone, and collected in a brief period of time, as sufficiently conclusive evidence in determining whether, or how much, factory labor is calculated to develop consumption. Were we to accept a favorite theory of medical men, that moisture and sudden atmospherical transitions are the most prolific causes of this disease, we should be almost justified in concluding, without any array of facts, that factory labor would induce it: as the operatives, in many departments, are occupied in rooms whose atmosphere is not only warm, but saturated with vapor; and, constantly perspiring, they emerge from this moist atmosphere, three or four times a day, into the cool air outside, and this, too generally, without the precaution of changing the dress, or adapting it to the transitions of temperature.

This theory must be received, however, with some allowance. Circumstances of this kind have a tendency to produce catarrhal and bronchial, rather than tubercular affections. Statistics of the extensive linen factories of Belfast, among the operatives in which the former class of diseases are found to predominate, show this to be the case; this fact was demonstrated also when comparing the amount of catarrhal and tubercular affections in our army and in the naval and land forces in the East Indies.

Whatever predominance of consumption more extended statistics might show to exist among operatives in cotton and woolen mills, should, perhaps, be attributed in a great part to the constrained and stooping positions which many of them are obliged to occupy, frequently to a want of proper exercise, and often owing to low rates of wages and failure of work, to poor food, and to badly ventilated and cared for houses.

In treating of the prevalence of consumption among the various callings, it may be remarked that I have omitted the statistics of the disease among a very numerous class of workmen, engaged particularly in the large manufactories of Birmingham and Sheffield, known as "dry grinders," who are employed in grinding upon dry stones, needles, forks, knives, &c. These workmen, as are also file-cutters, are subject to a species of consumption, so called, so malignant in its form, and so fearful in its extent, that almost all who adopt and pursue for a long time these occupations, fall victims to them. This disease has been treated of at full length by medical writers, and abundant statistics have been collected relative to its prevalence. None of these are, however, presented here, as the disease, while it is looked upon generally as genuine tubercular consumption, is, in reality, a species of bronchitis, induced by the irritation caused by the floating particles of steel which find admission into the lungs, and is characterized, not by the formation of tubercle, but by ulcerations extending from the large bronchial tubes to their terminations.

XV.—Comparative Prevalence of Consumption among the Two Sexes.

Whether consumption is most prevalent among males or females is a question on which a difference of opinion has always existed among medical writers. An abundant supply of facts shows conclusively that it causes a larger proportion of deaths among the latter sex. Of the numerous facts confirmative of this conclusion, the following may be cited:

Of 1554 patients who died of consumption in four of the French hospitals, 745 were men, and 809 women. We are told by Louis that, of a certain number of consumptive patients under his care, 57 were males and 70 females; and he confirms the deduction from this fact by the circumstance that, of forty individuals who died of various other chronic diseases, and whose lungs were found in a tuberculous condition, 15 were males and 25 females.

Still stronger confirmation of his opinion is found in a statement of M. de Chateauneuf, to the effect that, of the entire number of patients admitted into the Parisian Hospitals between the years 1821 and 1836, 26,055 were males, of whom 754 died of consumption, and 16,955 were females, of whom 809 died of the same disease—the excess being greatly on the side of the latter sex.

There died of consumption in England, in 1838, 27,935 males and 31,090 females; as the number of males in England that year was 7,668,245, and of females 7,885,615, the proportion of deaths from consumption among the two sexes was 36 males and 39 females, to every 10,000 inhabitants; while, according to the Irish census for 1841, there died from consumption in ten years 63,635 males and 71,955 females: the ratio, calculated in a manner similar to the one given above, being 15.8 males and 17.3 females to every 10,000 inhabitants—the relative proportion being about the same.

Of 247,419 deaths occurring from consumption in New-York, Philadelphia, Providence, England, Boston, Hamburg, Rouen, Naples, Geneva, Berlin, Sweden, and Paris, 116,527 were among the male, and 130,992 among the female sex.

Though consumption is, on the whole, more prevalent among females than males, certain writers maintain that, in large cities, it occurs more frequently in the former sex. This certainly is the case in some of the principal cities of England, though even in these, as we shall perceive, the statement does not admit of universal application.

Dr. Duncan states that while, of the general population of England and Wales, consumption would cause 378 deaths among every 100,000 males, it would cause 408 deaths among every 100,000 females; but, in the city of London, it would cause among the same number of males 451 deaths, and among the same number of females 377; and, in the city of Birmingham, 526 deaths among males and 410 among females.

The predominance of consumption among males in several of the English cities, is shown by the following table of the number of deaths by consumption occurring in every 100,000.

	MALES.	FEMALES.
Leeds	440	477
Birmingham	526	410
London	451	377
Liverpool and West Derby	595	571
Manchester and Salford	549	548
England and Wales	378	408

In the city of Leeds, as may be perceived, the excess is on the side of the females.

By the latest mortality reports of the city of London, the excess of consumption is still seen to be among the male sex, as I find that, of 308,318 deaths occurring in London among males, from 1847 to 1858, 1 death in every 8.2, or 12.17 per cent. of the whole, were caused by consumption; while of 300,357 deaths, during the same period, among females, it caused only 1 death in 9.2, or 10.18 per cent. of the whole.

An explanation of this excess of consumption among males in cities, over that which exists in the same sex in the country, has been offered in the fact that, in the city, men's passions are more excited and depressed—the failure of work, disappointed and over-wrought ambition, all have their due effect; while that mental tranquility so necessary to a sound body, is rarer than in the country—an explanation rational enough, so far as it goes, but by no means sufficient, inasmuch as, in the majority of cities generally, the excess of consumption is on the side of the female sex. A more reasonable supposition, I think, would be that, in the cities mentioned above—which are devoted almost exclusively to manufacturing or trading—the men are more subjected than in most cities to the deteriorating influences of bad air, confinement, and constrained and injurious positions attendant upon occupations in large factories, while, in Birmingham particularly, large numbers of workmen are exposed to danger from the effects of fine particles of iron and steel which are liable to enter the lungs—the deaths from diseases thus caused being generally classified in the reports as cases of consumption; and in London, aside from these influences, shopkeepers, particularly, do not enjoy the benefits of a free and pure atmosphere to so great an extent as they would in smaller cities. It has already been stated above, in speaking of the prevalence of consumption among various occupations, that a very large proportion of the tradesmen of London—not less than 28 per cent.—die of consumption. There are various other reasons, upon which I cannot at present touch, why the excess of consumption in London might be among males; certain it is that this excess, which has invariably existed for a large number of years, is not a mere accident, but has its origin in settled causes, to some of which is to be attributed a similar excess when it exists in other cities.

As may be seen, however, from the following table, constructed by Sir James Clarke, and derived from a large number of cases, the excess of consumption in cities generally is by no means constant on the side of either sex.

	CASES OF CONSUMPTION AMONG		PROPORTION AMONG	
	MALES.	FEMALES.	MALES.	FEMALES.
Hamburg......	555	445	10 to	8.7
Rouen (hospital population).	55	44	10 "	8.6
Naples........	382	315	10 "	8.2
New-York......	1,584	1,370	10 "	8.6
Geneva........	71	62	10 "	8.7
Berlin.........	328	292	10 "	8.8
Sweden	2,088	1,860	10 "	8.9
"	3,054	3,103	10 "	10.4
Berlin.........	560	655	10 "	11.6
Paris..........	2,219	2,970	10 "	13.3
"	3,965	5,579	10 "	14.3
Berlin (includ'g children)....	363	567	10 "	15.6

By this table, which was constructed a number of years ago, the excess of consumption among the two sexes is seen to vary at different periods and in different cities. In New-York the preponderance is shown to be on the side of the males, while at present it is on that of the females. The table, however, giving, as it does, merely the number of deaths from consumption among the two sexes, is of comparatively little value, as we are left in ignorance how much the excess of deaths among either sex might be due to the greater number of that sex among the general population.

In the city of Philadelphia, during a period of three years, among the males, 1 death in 9.81, or 10.18 per cent. of the deaths, was caused by consumption; among the females, 1 death in 8.28, or 12.07 per cent.

In the city of New-York, during the years 1848, '49, '50, '51, '53, '55, '56, and '58, the deaths from consumption were 21,567—the proportion among the males being 1 in 9.28, or 11 per cent., and, among the females, 1 in 8.23, or 12.4 per cent.

There are various circumstances which would lead us to suppose, *a priori*, that women would be more liable—in civilized countries particularly—to consumption than men; prominent among which are certain peculiarities of physical organization, and various habits of dress and life, which modern society has imposed upon its votaries.

Among the former may be mentioned the following, which are enumerated by the able Hufeland in treating of the physical peculiarities of the female:

"Great laxity of fibre: hence a disposition more to diseases of atony and relaxation.

"Quicker and richer chylification and sanguification; sanguification calculated to the nutrition of a second being; hence a plethoric state, a disposition to congestions.

"Greater productivity and plasticity: hence more inclination to abnormal productions, especially when the sexual production is interrupted or ceases."

We find, in these peculiarities, some of the principal conditions calculated to induce a fibrinous exudation into the lungs, which may afterwards become tubercle-corpuscles. According to Dr. James Hughes Bennett, of Edinburgh, in his "Monograph upon Pulmonary Tuberculosis"—the most reasonable and satisfactory explanation, to my own mind, that has yet been offered of the phenomena of consumption—tubercle is originally a simple exudation into the lungs of the *liquor sanguinis*, which, instead of progressing and becoming developed into perfect cells, forming normal or abnormal tissue, from its imperfect power of organization undergoes a retrograde metamorphosis, forming what are known as tubercle-corpuscles.

Obviously, therefore, for tubercular deposits to be formed, a certain condition of the blood and blood-vessels must exist, favoring exudation, and exudation must take place.

Without inquiring, at present, what the original cause is which induces these changes in the blood —which cause is at the foundation of the disease— it may simply be stated that the peculiarities of the female, noted by Hufeland, are such as favor these exudations. There is greater laxity of fibre, and a disposition more to diseases of atony and relaxation—hence to exudations. There is a plethoric state, a disposition to congestions, of which exudations are the usual sequence; greater plasticity, and, therefore, greater inclination to abnormal productions.

That all these circumstances have their weight in the development of diseases which are characterized by exudations, is shown by the fact that cancer—a formation in which the exudation goes on to a high degree of development—is much more frequent in females than in males, and that this disease, as well as consumption, is almost certain, if there is a tendency to either disease, to develop itself when the period of menstruation and child-bearing is over, after which period, a disposition to plethora of the blood-vessels is generated, from the circumstance that the system is no longer regularly relieved of a portion of its blood. Pregnancy, also, as is well known, will frequently prevent or arrest the development of consumption, and this, perhaps, from so great a portion of the blood being required for the nourishment of the fœtus.

I do not mean to be understood to assert that this rich condition of the blood and disposition to plethora are the most favorable that can exist for the production of tuberculous, though it may be of cancerous exudations; but it is more so than that condition of the blood and blood-vessels that ordinarily exists in men. On the contrary, a watery, impoverished condition of the blood-vessels is by far the most favorable to tubercular exudation: as it is exudation from blood in this condition that is most liable to sink into the low organization of tubercle—the rich plastic blood being most favorable to the development of the higher organization which exists in cancerous formations. Modern chemistry has, however, shown that woman's blood contains a smaller amount of globules and more water than that of man, and is, therefore, more easily deteriorated—an additional reason why consumption should be more prevalent among the female than the male sex.

Aside from these peculiarities of the female organization, there are numerous artificial causes which exercise a still more decided influence in the production of consumption among females.

Nor are we to place in the front rank of these causes, the domestic and in-door life which in most civilized countries is the habitual lot of women.

Valuable as is vigorous bodily exercise to the maintenance of health, the ordinary household avocations of woman, regularly pursued, are quite as satisfactory to the requirements of her health as the more violent labor of man to his; unless, indeed, we coincide with those energetic ladies who maintain that masculine occupations are better adapted to woman than her own. Nature has so constructed her and ordered her life that she is not fitted for violent bodily labor: she is weaker, her bones and limbs are smaller and more delicately formed, her temperament is more lymphatic, she has more fat and less muscle, is less energetic and capable of enduring fatigue than man, and, during a great part of her existence, she is incapacitated, by peculiar physical conditions and the duties of maternity, from severe bodily labor. It is stated that, in certain parts of France and Belgium—where a great part of the out-door labor is performed by women—they are no more subject to consumption than men. Nevertheless, while a *greater* immunity from consumption may be gained by women (as by men) by additional exercise, it is still true that, so far as the disease in question is concerned, women will enjoy, in the regular exercise of their ordinary avocations, *ceteris paribus*, their normal degree of health. *Per contra*, the gain in health which women on the Continent acquire, by their masculine labors, is counter-balanced by the roughening and distortion of their womanly *physique*.

Prominent among the artificial causes above referred to as calculated to favor the development of consumption among women, may be mentioned the habit of constricting the lower part of the chest by tight lacing, by which the action of the lower part of the lungs is impaired and confined, and the burden of respiration, and more than a normal proportion of blood, is thrown upon the upper lobes, the favorite seat of tuberculous deposits —a tendency to stagnation, congestion, and exudation being thereby induced in those parts; and the habit of leaving the upper part of the chest, the vital part in phthisis pulmonalis, exposed, too often without regard to the condition of the atmosphere, under the impression that these parts are strengthened by exposure to the weather.

Some common habits of life, and Fashion—a queen pitiless to her too devoted subjects, in her rule, and, like Moloch, oft "besmeared with sacrifice of human blood"—furnish no small number of victims to this disease. Days passed in idleness, in perusing books not promoting tranquil or healthy thought, but ministering to the less noble qualities of the imagination, in languid employment or unrefreshing exercise, and eccentricities of diet abhorrent to all reason,—betray themselves too often, in our American ladies particularly, in the narrow and contracted chest, the inelastic step, and disorders of deranged nutrition, the latter, generally, the *fons et origo* of tubercular diseases; while thin shoes and damp walks, balls and parties following close upon each other, with their accompaniments of heated rooms alternating with chilling draughts, indigestible suppers at unnatural hours, unrefreshing sleep by day-light and wakefulness at night, a complete revolution in short, of nature's laws, present an array of external circumstances than which more favorable to the development of consumption can scarcely be imagined.

Ritchie, in his descriptions appended to Turner's "Rivers of France," states that, in the Arrondissement of Nantes alone, three hundred and seventeen unmarried girls, from the age of sixteen to twenty-two, die every year, and two hundred and forty young married women, from the age of twenty to thirty-two! These, with few exceptions, are the victims of the "*bal.*" He says, describing the French *bal:* "It often takes place under a thin canopy, and the tired *danseuse* sits down to look at the others, unconscious of her danger. If the scene has been a room, she lingers in the cold air on coming out to bid good night. We have often ourselves seen a company of young girls crouching under a canvass roof, loth to be driven away by a shower, receiving the rain-drops as they fell upon their glowing bosoms with a playful scream, and inhaling, with the unconsciousness of lambs in the steaming den of the butcher, that damp, chill, heavy atmosphere in which the germs of consumption were as thick as moths in the sunbeam."

Unlike as our festivities are to these, the effects are often the same; and, too often, alas! perishing in the unrelenting grasp of consumption, do we meet their victims, whose unhappy fate Victor Hugo describes in lines so pathetic and beautiful, that I hope to be pardoned for giving them, even in a statistical paper:

> "Quels tristes lendemains laisse le bal folâtre!
> Adieu parure, et danse, et rires enfantins!

Aux chansons succédait la toux opiniâtre ;
Aux plaisir, rose et frais, la fièvre au teint bleuâtre,
  Aux yeux brillans, les yeux éteints.
  * * * *
Elle est morte. A quinze ans, belle, heureuse, adorée !
  * * * *

"Joyeuse, et d'une main ravie,
Elle allait, moissonnant les roses de la vie,
  Beauté, plaisir, jeunesse, amour !
La pauvre enfant, de fête en fête promenée,
  De ce bouquet charmant arrangeait les couleurs !
Mais qu'elle est passé vite ; helas ! l'infortunée,
Ainsi qu' Orphelia, par le fleuve entraînée,
  Elle est morte en cueillant des fleurs !"

XVI.—Its Prevalence at Different Ages of Life.

It it stated by Hippocrates, that the period of life at which the greatest mortality from consumption occurs is between the ages of 20 and 35 years. All modern statistics are confirmatory of this statement, as all show the greatest number of deaths to occur between the twentieth and thirtieth year.

The proportion of deaths at the various periods of life is shown by the following table, taken from the "Géographie et Statistiques Médicales" of M. Boudin.

Total number of deaths from consumption in England and Wales, in 1847: 53,317; divided as follows:

AGES.	DEATHS.	PER CENT.
Under 5 years	5,195	9.7
5 to 10 "	1,656	3.1
10 " 15 "	2,342	4.4
15 " 20 "	5,526	10.4
20 " 25 "	7,420	13.9

AGES.	DEATHS.	PER CENT.
25 to 30 years	6,666	12.5
30 " 35 "	5,467	10.2
35 " 40 "	4,757	9.0
40 " 45 "	3,750	7.3
45 " 50 "	2,938	5.5
50 " 55 "	2,372	4.4
55 " 60 "	1,899	3.5
60 " 65 "	1,464	2.7
65 " 70 "	1,020	2.0
70 " 75 "	449	0.9
75 " 80 "	237	0.4
80 " 85 "	67	0.1
85 " 90 "	19	0.04
90 " 95 "	5	0.005
95 and over	18	0.03

Of a table constructed by myself, of 88,427 deaths from consumption, occurring in both sexes, in various cities and countries, there occurred between the ages of 20 and 30, the ten years in which the number of deaths was greatest, 22,554; between the ages of 30 and 40, the next most fatal period, 18,152.

Between 10 and 20	11,093
" 40 " 50	10,932
From birth to 10 years of age . .	9,605

Between	50	and	60	. . . .	6,886
"	60	"	70	. . . .	5,745
"	70	"	80	. . . .	1,178
"	80	"	90	. . . .	194
"	90	"	100	. . . .	33

Thus we see that the liability to the disease is greatest between the ages of 20 and 30, after which period it becomes less and less as we advance in life; though, as we have seen by this table, it is somewhat greater between the tenth and twentieth than between the fortieth and fiftieth year.

It has been variously stated by writers, that consumption is developed at an earlier age among females than among males. The following table, which I have constructed, shows that this is not true before the tenth year; yet, between that time and the forty-fifth year, the various decades furnish a greater per-centage of deaths among the females than the males; but that, after the forty-fifth year, the per-centage is greater among the males.

Deaths occurring from Consumption in England, from 1848 *to* 1852, *in* 1856, *and in London in* 1857.

MALES. TOTAL DEATHS FROM CONSUMPTION: **193,729.**		**FEMALES.** TOTAL DEATHS FROM CONSUMPTION: **216,133.**
	MALES.	FEMALES.
Under 5 years of age.........	15,857 or 8 4 per cent.	15,111 or 6.9 per cent.
Between 5 and 10 years	5,440 .. 2.8 ..	6,116 .. 2.8 ..
.. 10 .. 15	6,670 .. 3.4 ..	10,852 .. 5.0 ..
.. (5 .. 15)	12,110 .. 6.2 ..	16,968 .. 7.8 ..
.. 15 .. 25	44,423 .. 22.92 ..	56,515 .. 26.1 ..
.. 25 .. 35	43,791 .. 22.6 ..	53,965 .. 24.9 ..
.. 35 .. 45	32,890 .. 16.9 ..	36,795 .. 17.0 ..
.. 45 .. 55	23,244 .. 11.9 ..	20,534 .. 9.5 ..
.. 55 .. 65	13,903 .. 7.0 ..	11,448 .. 5.2 ..
.. 65 .. 75	5,862 .. 3.0 ..	4,773 .. 2.2 ..
.. 75 .. 85	867 .. 0.45 ..	901 .. 0.41 ..
.. 85 .. 95	59 .. 0.02 ..	84 .. 0.03 ..

Various explanations have been given, of the greater tendency of consumption to develop itself among females than among males, during the period above mentioned, all of which are far from being satisfactory. Perhaps as rational an explanation as can be adduced, may be found in the fact that the physical peculiarities, which I have mentioned as being characteristic of the female sex, are most strongly marked at this period—the period of womanhood, and in the circumstance that it is at this time that the habits of social life above enumerated exercise their greatest influence.

There are many other points connected with the existence and course of consumption, relative to which statistics might be given, but upon which I have at present neither time nor space to enter. Among these may be mentioned the statistics of the duration of the disease; of the results of treatment; of the cases in which hæmorrhages occur; of the different lungs and different parts of the lungs affected; statistics of its hereditariness; and more extended statistics of its prevalence in regions in which intermittent fevers prevail. These points I hope to make the subject of consideration in a future paper.

XVII.—Conclusions.

From the various facts I have presented, the following conclusions may be deduced:

I.—That, if climate be incapable, *per se*, of generating consumption, it is one of the most powerful agents in modifying and controlling its prevalence.

II.—That there are certain varieties of climate inimical to the development of consumption, and of these the most unfavorable, are:

1. Those characterized by extreme and unvarying cold.
2. Those climates characterized by a cool, dry atmosphere.
3. Those which have a very high temperature, with but a moderate amount of moisture.

III.—That the climates most favorable to the development and existence of consumption, are:

1. Those which have a high temperature and a moist atmosphere.
2. Moist climates with a moderate temperature.
3. Climates characterized by great variations in the daily temperature.

Finally, with regard to climate, humidity seems most favorable, and dryness most unfavorable to consumption, though a moist salt air is not calculated to develop it.

IV.—That the liability to consumption is increased by insufficient exercise, by occupations which require such positions as constrict the chest, by impure and confined air, by improper or insufficient food, and by influences which have a depressing effect upon the mind.

V.—That a long continuance either of light or darkness will not produce it.

VI.—That it is more prevalent on land than on the sea.

VII.—That it is more prevalent among females than among males, and, finally,

VIII.—That the period of its greatest mortality is between the ages of twenty and thirty years.

TO PHYSICIANS!

Recently Published by Wm. RADDE, 300 Broadway.

A

MONOGRAPH ON ACONITE.

ITS USES:

TOGETHER WITH ACCURATE STATEMENTS DERIVED FROM THE VARIOUS SOURCES OF MEDICAL LITERATURE.

TRANSLATED FROM THE GERMAN OF DR. REIL,

BY HENRY B. MILLARD, M. D., A. M.

Price .... $0.75.—With Colored Plate.... $1.00.

The above production has received, since its translation, the highest expressions of commendation from physicians and medical journals of both systems of medicine, and may be regarded as the classic work upon the subject of which it treats.

Of the seventeen Monographs upon Aconite—published in Latin, German, English, and Italian (including the valuable treatise of Fleming), between 1761 and 1861—this is by far the fullest and most complete, and presents all that has yet been ascertained of the physiological and therapeutic action of this valuable remedy. The author, well known as one of the ablest physiological writers of Germany, has treated his subject with equal ability and impartiality, and has included the most important and valuable uses and experience, as furnished by physicians of both schools.

An idea of the thoroughness and impartiality of the work may be conveyed by the following—

TABLE OF CONTENTS.

From numerous favorable notices of medical journals we present only the following:

This Monograph—probably the best which has ever been published upon the subject—has been translated and given to the public by Dr. Millard, of New-York. Apart from the intrinsic value of the work, which is well known to all German medical scholars, the translation of it has been completed in the most thorough and pains-taking way; and all the Latin and Greek quotations have been carefully rendered into English.

The book itself is a work of great merit—thoroughly exhausting the whole range of the subject. To obtain a thorough view of the spirit of the action of the drug, we can recommend no better work.—*North American Journal of Homœopathy.*

After a careful examination of this treatise, we find it full and complete on the subject of which it treats. The bibliography of the subject, the medical history of the plant, the results of original investigations and experiments made with a view of testing its properties, the several accidental experiences obtained from various writers respecting its poisonous action, are all fully detailed. The author collates the testimony from any and every source, examines critically its relative weight, sifts out whatever seems erroneous or unconclusive, and concludes with a *resumé* of the real value of Aconite as a remedy.

We consider this "prize essay" as presenting, in a high degree, the great advantages flowing from special treatises devoted exclusively to one theme. The search for information bearing upon it is almost exhaustive; it is, consequently, rich in facts for those desiring to be fully informed. Text-books and general treatises do very well for beginners, or for those who take only a general interest in the multifarious questions of which they are expected to treat; but to those who wish a thorough knowledge upon any one article, treatises exclusively devoted to their consideration must, of course, always prove more satisfactory.—*Charleston Medical Journal and Review.*

www.ingramcontent.com/pod-product-compliance
Lightning Source LLC
LaVergne TN
LVHW021427110826
845150LV00007B/2124

* 9 7 8 1 4 2 5 5 0 7 7 6 3 *